OLIVER TREANOR

Mother of the Redeemer, Mother of the Redeemed

Mother of the Redeemer, Mother of the Redeemed

OLIVER TREANOR

with a foreword by
Dr John Magee, Bishop of Cloyne

CHRISTIAN CLASSICS

FOUR COURTS PRESS

The typesetting of this book was
input by Gilbert Gough Typesetting, Dublin
in Paladium, for Four Courts Press Ltd,
Kill Lane, Blackrock, Co. Dublin,
and Christian Classics, Inc., P.O. Box 30, Westminster,
Maryland 21157, USA.

BRITISH LIBRARY CATALOGUING IN PUBLICATION DATA

Treanor, Oliver
Mother of the Redeemer, Mother of the redeemed.
1. Mary, *Mother of Jesus Christ*
I. Title
232.91   BT602

ISBN 1-85182-034-5

ACKNOWLEDGEMENTS

Chapters 1 and 2 of this book were first published in *L'Osservatore Romano*
(English edition), (24 August 1987) and *Religious Life Review* (January-February
1988), respectively.

Made and printed in Great Britain by
The Guernsey Press Co. Ltd., Guernsey, Channel Islands.

Adam is set free
and Eve dances for joy,
and in spirit they cry aloud to thee,
O Theotokos,
'By thee, through Christ's appearance,
we are delivered
from Adam's ancient curse.'

ORTHODOX LITURGY

Contents

Abbreviations

LG	Dogm. Const. *Lumen gentium*
UR	Decree *Unitatis redintegratio*
MC	Enc. *Marialis cultus*
SC	Const. *Sacrosanctum concilium*
RM	Enc. *Redemptoris Mater*

Foreword

Any treatise on the role of Mary, the Virgin Mother of Nazareth, in the working out of the 'divine mystery of salvation' must necessarily situate her in relationship to the Redeemer on the one hand and to the Redeemed on the other. And so the title given to this book by Father Oliver Treanor is truly aptly chosen: 'Mother of the Redeemer, Mother of the Redeemed'.

In order to understand the role of Mary in relationship to the Redeemer and to the Redeemed one has to come to understand Mary's role in the mystery of Christ and in the mystery of the Church. Father Treanor has given us a most valuable exposition in this work, tracing for us the role of Mary in the plan of salvation as understood in Sacred Scripture and in the Fathers and as clearly enunciated for us in the teaching of the Second Vatican Council in its Dogmatic Constitution on the Church *Lumen gentium*. Following on this basic teaching on the Church we are drawn into a Marian comprehension of the Church in which the redeemed are caught up in the 'communio' which is truly trinitarian and which is offered to us through the readiness of Mary to become the 'handmaid of the Lord'. The Church, which becomes, in us, the very extension of the 'communio' which exists in the intimate being of the Triune God, responds to this

God-sharing action in Christ through its liturgical life, and at the heart of this liturgical activity is found She who through her very existence within the body of the Church, as Mother, renders praise, glory and thanks to God 'for the great things He has wrought in her'. Mary, then, is at the heart of the liturgical life of the Church and renders it meaningful. Father Treanor elucidates this aspect of the life of the Church in his exposition of the post-conciliar document of Pope John Paul VI *Marialis cultus*.

In this Marian Year, which in itself is an extended 'Advent' in preparation for the great Christological celebration at the end of this millenium of the two thousand years since the Incarnation in the womb of Mary of the Saviour, we have been invited to contemplate the 'pilgrim' par excellence, Mary, the Mother of Christ and of all mankind, and to come to know and appreciate the major role she plays in the work of salvation. In his encyclical letter *Redemptoris Mater* Pope John Paul has shared with the whole Church the richness of Church teaching combined with the depth of his own personal Marian devotion. I have read with deep interest Father Treanor's treatment of this latest Papal teaching on the role of Mary and I find it truly sensitive and challenging. I myself, who have lived with both Paul VI and John Paul II and have served them intimately as personal Secretary, must state that Father Treanor has penetrated deeply into their understanding of the nature of the Church and of the role of the Mother of the Redeemer in the overall plan of salvation. Knowing them intimately myself and having shared with them in their own spiritual lives, I would say, without hesitation, that it would be their ardent wish that during this Marian Year there be brought forth in the Church a great spiritual fruit, namely the dual devotion, Eucharistic and Marian. This is indeed now happening in the Marian shrines throughout the world. May it spread in every ecclesial community and may it be that which will give birth to a truly genuine ecumenical spirit in the Church. For it is the Eucharist which makes the Church and which calls her into one, and in the words of Cardinal Ratzinger 'only in being Marian do we become Church'.

I am truly grateful to Father Oliver for sharing with us his understanding of the place of Mary in the mystery of Christ and of the Church. May all those who are privileged to read these pages be opened to the richness of the Triune God who found a ready handmaid in Mary to share with mankind that life which is all-embracing and everlasting.

+ *John Magee*, Bishop of Cloyne
1 JANUARY 1988

Mary in the post-conciliar Church

Vatican II, the Council of *aggiornamento* and *rinnovamento*, places Mary firmly in the forefront of renewal by devoting an entire chapter to her in the Dogmatic Constitution on the Church. Reappraising the Virgin's role in the plan of salvation the document strikes a fine balance between what it calls 'all false exaggeration', on the one hand, and 'too summary an attitude' to Mariology on the other (LG 67). To maintain this balance requires a proper understanding of who our Lady is, and what she has been called to do. Ultimately Mary's vocation is identical with that of the Church: she leads men to Christ the Redeemer. In doing so she draws our attention to the sacramental nature of revelation, showing us God's love through the humanity of her Son. Herself totally united to the Word made flesh, she manifests that love also through her own tender compassion as Mother of God and mother of all God's people. What was formerly above and beyond our reach she has brought close within our grasp in a very human way, giving it visibility and shape (1 Jn 1:1-2). Mary is therefore to be regarded as a crucial instrument of God's purpose in guiding us to a true knowledge of himself. For its part, the Council's great contribution to Marian renewal is that it sets before us a clear and authentic teaching, based on scripture and church tradition, that affirms the necessity of Mary in God's saving initiative and in the faith-response of the Christian life.

Why does the Church venerate the Virgin Mary?

This question is asked by many Catholics today as well as Protestants. In the context of the conciliar teaching the answer is threefold. First of all we venerate the Virgin in imitation of God himself who honoured her more highly than we ever could, by choosing her to be the Mother of his Son. Our filial respect for her cannot exceed his who in all things sets the example that we must follow. Secondly, we honour Mary in keeping with the long and consistent practice of the people of God. Both the Old and New Testaments acclaim her — the Old by way of anticipation, the New by way of fulfilment. From the beginning of *Genesis* to the last book of the bible Mary is either prefigured or portrayed as the handmaid of God's wisdom, the focus of mankind's hopes and aspirations, the cause of our joy and consolation. It is not only the hallowed witness of scripture that invites and approves our filial confidence in her. It is also the fact of the ancient and unbroken pattern of prayer which has always reflected the doctrinal creeds and symbols of the believing community. The oldest Marian prayer we know of, for example, dates from around 250 A.D., the time of the early persecutions. Emerging from the anguish of a tortured people it attests an already established devotion to the *Theotokos*, Mary's primary title (in which she was confirmed by the Council of Ephesus some two centuries later):

Sub tuum praesidium confugimus,
sancta Dei Genetrix;
nostras deprecationes ne despicias in
    necessitatibus,
sed a periculis cunctis libera nos semper,
Virgo gloriosa et benedicta.

Discovered in Egypt in 1917 on papyrus measuring seven by nearly four inches (now housed in the John Rylands Library, Manchester), the original ten lines of Greek, translated literally, read:

Under cover of your motherly heart
we flee for refuge, Mother of God;
do not brush aside our entreaties in our stress,
but rescue us from danger,
you, peerlessly holy and blessed.[1]

Contemporary frescoes in the burial chambers of the Roman catacombs of Priscilla depict the Virgin Mother, enthroned, with the Child on her lap. From this we can assume a very real appreciation of Mary's soteriological significance in the post-apostolic era, and a lively cult of confidence in the power of her maternal intercession.

Finally, we honour Mary today under the impulse of the Holy Spirit, promised and sent by Jesus to guide his members in the way of all truth. He it is who enables us to understand the deposit of faith entrusted first to Mary and through her to the apostolic Church.

As Seat of Wisdom and Spouse of the Spirit she is still the Temple and Guardian of Truth. To be close to her is to be faithful to the on-going renewal of Church life and worship of which the Paraclete is the principle, and the primary cause.

13

Theotokos and Vatican II

The Mother of God perfectly exemplifies the spirit and inspiration of Vatican II's efforts to update Catholic faith in the modern world. Three characteristics differentiate the sixteen documents from other statements of the past. They were consciously Christocentric in their approach. Their context, moreover, was specifically ecclesiological, that is, related to a carefully studied theology of Church that goes beyond former constitutional theory. And lastly Vatican II saw itself as a pastoral council, the first of its kind. Its fundamental aim was to minister to the twentieth century, not simply to react polemically against spiritual indifference or religious heresy. Against this background the Virgin Mary stands as a figure that represents the Council itself. Her function too is to hold Christ up to the gaze of today's world; to reaffirm the nature and function of the Church as the sacrament of salvation open to all men and ready for dialogue; and to inspire by her own example in the gospels a fresh pastoral zeal among laity and clergy alike in service of the kingdom. To understand Mary, therefore, is to understand the challenge of the Council's teaching. By the same token, to study the Council's spirit is to know the spirit of Mary. God speaks through both as through one.

Mary and the Holy Trinity

Her very name, derived from an Egyptian term meaning 'beloved', bespeaks Mary's relationship with the triune God to whom she is all things. To the Father, she is a beloved daughter; to the Son, a beloved Mother; to the

Spirit, beloved bride. Co-operating fully with the divine will at each stage of its unfolding in salvation history, Mary is caught up and centred in the heart of the Trinity. Through faith and humble obedience she is awarded perfect communion with Love itself. That Love she brought into the world by her voluntary participation in the sacred missions of the second and third divine Persons. At the Annunciation her consent made possible the body of Christ, the historical Jesus. At Pentecost she was present when the Spirit descended a second time, bringing forth the body of Christ, the Church. Between those two great axes of God's activity, her life comprised several missionary journeys (to Elizabeth's house, to Bethlehem, into Egypt, back to Nazareth, to Jerusalem, to Cana and to Calvary) that were enriched by her prayer of contemplation, and of petition for others. Like the sacred liturgy of the Church, Mary's entire orientation was trinitarian. How appropriate then was Pope Paul VI's observation in 1974 that 'it is supremely fitting that exercises of piety towards the Virgin Mary should clearly express the trinitarian ... note that is intrinsic and essential to them, (since) Christian worship in fact is of itself worship offered ... to the Father, through Christ, in the Spirit" (*MC* 25).

First disciple, first apostle of Christ

Every Mariological statement is actually a statement about Christ. To speak of her motherhood is to affirm the humanity taken by the Word for the salvation of the world. To celebrate Mary's virginity is to declare faith in Jesus' divine nature, conceived as he was by the power of the Spirit. To acknowledge her assumption is to admit Christ's Lordship over sin and death, and to say with St Paul: 'Christ has been raised from the dead, the first fruits of those who have fallen asleep. . . . As in Adam all die, so also in Christ shall all be made alive. But each in his own order: Christ the first fruits, then at his coming those who belong to Christ' (1 Cor 15:20, 22-23). Mary verifies the Word. Her life and glorification are an exegesis of scripture, a clarification of the meaning of her Son's work and what he has accomplished. It is an amazing but true observation that the Virgin never appears in the bible other than in the company of her Son. Such intimate association with him confirms her raison d'etre — to be first his disciple in following him, to be then his apostle in proclaiming him. Through her actions and her words, by her silences and by what she is our Lady imparts to us the conviction of faith both existentially and ontologically. Where she is reflected upon through the gospels Jesus becomes truly present because of her, in the heart of the listener. Of the holy union of the sacred hearts of Jesus and Mary, we can repeat with the Marian poet:

> Here all is perfect speech of heart to Heart;
> Here are no words, but fulness of the Word.

Our Lady and the unity of the Church

Since Mary is the Church's first member and its model, her concern is for its welfare in every respect but particularly for its unity. In this ecumenical age, and especially for Catholics in the wake of the Council's Decree on Ecumenism (*Unitatis redintegratio*), the effort

16

to bring about visible communion among Christians finds its strongest encouragement in the Mother of God. Her proximity to Christ is the very criterion advocated by the Council Fathers (later echoed by Pope John Paul II) for achieving unity, the goal for which her Son gave his life on the cross. Hence UR 20 proclaims 'Christ as the source and centre of ecclesiastical communion', a conviction also close to the heart of the Faith and Order Movement: 'It has been proved true that as we seek to draw closer to Christ, we come closer to one another' (Lund, 1952). The Virgin Mother of the Church gives us the lead in this ideal. Because she sums up in herself what the Church is, her union with Christ is a challenge and a prophetic sign to Christian communities everywhere. To the ecumenically lukewarm, her Christocentrism is a reminder that division is incompatible with love for Christ. To those who labour for ecclesial re-unification, it is a promise of success since unity comes from God who will in fact gather his faithful into one at the end of time. In that eschatological communion, the blessed — like Mary herself — will be those who listened to the Word, 'that all might be one', and worked for its fulfilment on earth. To be in the Church, therefore, is to be with Mary in her inseparable union with her Son. To be apart from her is to be estranged from the Church as a Communion. In her, who is our Mother the Church, abides the entire means towards perfect integrity, namely, the grace and peace of God our Father and the Lord Jesus Christ, and the fellowship of the Holy Spirit. Blessed Isaac of Stella articulates Mary's ecclesial identity in the most eloquent manner:

Christ, Head and Body is one, whole and unique; but this one Christ is of one God in heaven and one mother on earth; this Christ is both many sons and one son. For as Head and Body are one son and many sons, so Mary and the Church are one mother and many; one virgin and many.

Each is mother, each is virgin; both conceive in holiness from the same Spirit; both bring forth a child without sin for God the Father. Mary gave birth to the absolutely sinless Head for the Body; the Church gave birth, in the forgiveness of every sin, to the Body for the Head. Each is mother of Christ, but neither without the other gives birth to the whole Christ.

And so in the divinely inspired scriptures, what is said in general of the Virgin Mother the Church is said individually of the Virgin Mary; and what is said in the particular case of the Virgin Mother Mary is rightly understood of the Virgin Mother Church universally; and when mention is made of either, it is to be understood almost indifferently and conjointly of both (Sermon 51).

Our Lady can truthfully be called Patroness of the Ecumenical Movement. As prototype of the Church and Mother of the Church's Head she accommodates, in the unity of the Spirit, all who come to God through her. As the heavenly Jerusalem, our Mother in glory, she also foreshadows what the Church is to become at the *eschaton*. Therefore, for all who are committed to unity, Mary is the exemplar, the pledge and the guarantee of that perfect oneness with God which the Church already possesses in mystery and will one day manifest in glory when it appears, together with our Lady herself, as the *Communio Sanctorum*.

1 Translation made by J.P. Kenny, SJ, in his *The Meaning of Mary for Modern Man* (Melbourne 1980), 123.

Mary in the plan of salvation (Lumen gentium, *Chapter 8*)

I. INTRODUCTION: LG 52-54

Exposition

'The divine mystery of salvation' can be summed up in one phrase — unity-with-God. It was for this that the Word became flesh and established his Church on earth. By the incarnation Jesus took to himself all that is human and joined it to all that is God. Inaugurating the Church which is his body he ensured that mankind's communion with the Father would continue in his faithful members. In planning this God counted on Mary's co-operation. Mother of Christ our Head, she is intimately one with the Holy Trinity. As mother of Christ's members, she is 'also united to all those who are to be saved'. Her singular value in God's eyes and her involvement in our redemption mean that she is most worthy of honour.

With this doctrine in mind the aim of the Dogmatic Constitution is to set forth 'both the role of the Blessed Virgin in the mystery of the Incarnate Word and the Mystical Body, and the duties of the redeemed towards the Mother of God, who is mother of Christ and mother of men, and most of all those who believe'.

Reflection

Lumen gentium's last chapter, on our Lady, returns to the theme with which the document opened, that of 'mystery'. This is a key term in the Council's understanding of the Church. It underscores the starting-point of ecclesiology today, which begins by considering not the hierarchical or juridical features of the Church's earthly form, but God himself who manifests his invisible nature in the life of the visible community of love. Jesus did not simply found the Church, he revealed it. The *ekklesia* existed before time began. As St Cyprian says, the Church is that 'unity of the Father and the Son and the Holy Spirit' which pre-dates creation and into which all flesh is drawn through the mystery of the incarnation. When St Paul used the word in its Greek form, *musterion*, he meant the secret plan of salvation, which was 'hidden for ages and generations but (is) now made manifest to the saints', namely 'Christ in you' (Col 1:26, 27). This is the reality towards which everything in the Church is orientated — her structures, her preaching, her magisterial authority, her sacraments and worship, her charisms, her diocesan organization and parish life.

Sometimes we can forget this. One aspect of Church may take on undue importance for us over the rest. We can lose sight of the ultimate purpose of the work we do, the building of the unity of the members with Christ. Perhaps the work itself can become more necessary than the people it is intended to serve. It is even possible to stop speaking of Christ to them altogether. When this happens, it is Mary who leads us back to the reality of the mystery. *Lumen gentium* locates her, as mother, at the centre of the Father's hidden plan which he revealed not just through what Mary *did*, but even more through what she *is*. Living in the company of God she epitomizes what the Church actually is and, therefore, what it is called to be — a holy communion with heaven on earth. In her maternal company we can lay aside the idols of our misconceptions about the Church as we would like it to be, and learn to re-discover its real nature and function according to the mind of God himself. At a conference in Italy in 1985, Cardinal Ratzinger explained the relationship between Mary, the Church and the mystery in this way:

> The Church is not an apparatus; she is not simply an institution; she is not even one among many sociological entities; she is a person. She is a woman. She is mother. She is living. The Marian comprehension of the Church most decisively counters a merely organizational and bureaucratic concept of the Church. We cannot *make* the Church, we must *be* her. And only to the extent that faith, beyond our *doings*, moulds our *being*, are we Church, is the Church within us. Only in being Marian do we become Church. Even in the beginning, the Church was not made but generated. She was generated when in the soul of Mary there awakened the *fiat*. This is the most profound desire of the Council: that the Church awaken in our souls. Mary shows us the way.[2]

II. THE FUNCTION OF THE BLESSED VIRGIN IN THE PLAN OF SALVATION: LG 55-59

Exposition

A synopsis of Mary's role in the mystery of salvation falls into three chronological sections — from Genesis to the Immaculate Conception; the period of the gospels; and from Pentecost to the Assumption. For its sources Vatican II draws on the Old and New Testament scriptures, the sacred tradition of the early Fathers and the magisterial teaching from Chalcedon in the fifth century, to Pius XII.

Allusions to Mary in the Old Testament occur in the context of the Messianic Promise. Beginning a thousand years before Christ, the sacred writers envisage 'the figure of a woman, the mother of the Redeemer, in a gradually clearer light' as time goes by. A cryptic reference made after the Fall to the seed of Eve whose offspring would crush the serpent's seed (Gen 3:15) soon crystallizes into the virgin of the Immanuel passage in *Isaiah*, and the mysterious 'one who is to give birth' in the Bethlehem prediction of Micah. All is made clear in the opening chapter of the New Testament when Matthew depicts Jesus' conception and birth from Mary as the perfect fulfilment of Jewish prophecy.

Reflecting on the depth of the mystery here, the early Fathers see the Virgin as the new Eve: not just 'mother of all who live' (Gen 3:20), but Mother of Life itself, of him 'who renews all things'. Collaborating with the new Adam, Mary helps her Son to reverse the pride and disobedience of the first Eve through her exceptional 'faith and obedience' as the handmaid of the Lord. Hence the

24

Fathers honour Mary's immaculate origin, enriched as she was 'from the first moment of her conception with the splendour of an entirely unique holiness ... free from every stain of sin', and fittingly hailed as 'full of grace'.

In the gospels 'this union of the mother with the Son in the work of salvation is made manifest from the time of Christ's virginal conception up to his death'. Through what we normally call the joyful mysteries of the infancy narratives (*Luke* and *Matthew*), she plays a leading role in bringing Christ to others. As his disciple from Cana to Calvary she witnesses his miracles and listens to his preaching, pondering his words in her heart and uniting herself to his suffering. At the foot of the cross she completes her 'pilgrimage of faith' by offering him lovingly to the Father and accepting in exchange, at the request of the dying Jesus, the beloved disciple as her son.

Finally, at the outpouring of the Holy Spirit, when God's plan was brought to its fullest manifestation, Mary was present in prayer in the midst of the church community. She who was twice overshadowed by the Paraclete now reigns with Christ in his glory. Having been assumed body and soul immaculate into heaven, she is 'fully conformed to her Son, the Lord of Lords and conqueror of sin and death'.

In this section the Council uses the terms 'mystery' or 'plan' (which mean the same thing) no less than seven times. By this fact we are meant to see Mary's function in the scheme of salvation as a matter of the greatest theological importance for a proper understanding of God's work on our behalf in Christ, in the Holy Spirit, and in the Church.

Reflection

When the dogma of the Immaculate Conception was defined in 1854 a great statue of our Lady was erected in Rome's Piazza di Spagna to celebrate the occasion. It is flanked by four figures from the Old Testament who anticipated her in their prophetic works — Moses (the Pentateuch), David (the psalms), Isaiah and Micah. The tableau recalls the Virgin's title, 'Queen of Prophets'. Here is one who assures us that God is faithful to all the promises made from the start of salvation history. In the words of St Luke, 'Blessed is she who believed that the promise made to her would be fulfilled (1:45). Mary's very existence testifies that God is in control of his creation and of all time, past, present and future. No matter how disastrous man's mistakes, God's predetermined plan runs true to its course. Those mistakes in fact even enhance his designs. They have been incorporated into the scheme of redemption, as the Easter *Exultet* proclaims on Holy Saturday night — 'O *felix* culpa'. As Mother of the Promised Redeemer, our Lady's first role is to give witness that those who put their trust in God will not be disappointed. This is a message we need to hear clearly in the modern age. Young people especially need to hear it: their discouragement can be intense when they see evil gaining its own way in the world. As one who understands her Son's words, 'Be not afraid, I have overcome the world', Mary Queen of Prophets inspires a serene and sure optimism in the God of the impossible and the ultimate victory of his plan.

The Immaculate Virgin was capable of great faith and hope because she was one of God's poor. From ancient times the poor have always been a force for good in the mystery of salvation. Known in the Old Testament as the *'anawim Yahweh*, they were remarkable for their total reliance on divine providence. Poverty was their greatest asset, for it enabled Yahweh to accomplish through them all he had in mind to do. Mary is a child of their faith; she springs from their stock. Even before she was born her spirit dwelt among the *'anawim*, leading them forward in prophecy and in promise, enclosing the hope of Israel in her womb. It is their constancy and its Marian fruitfulness that we remember in the liturgy on the feast of Our Lady's parents (27 July):

> They are Israelites: they were made God's sons; from them, in natural descent, sprang the Messiah (Rom 9:4-5; vespers).

> Let us praise . . . our ancestors in their successive generations. . . . In their descendants there remains a rich inheritance born of them. Their descendants stand by the covenants, and, thanks to them, so do their children's children. Their offspring will last forever, their glory will not fade (Sir 44:4-5; from the Mass).

Mary is the Virgin of the Poor in every generation. For them she continues to bring God's promise to fulfilment through the womb of the Church's sacramental life. Wherever the new prophecy of the gospel is proclaimed she is still in our midst, affirming by her own glory now as Queen of heaven, that blessed indeed are 'the poor in spirit, for theirs is the kingdom'.

In Mary the Old and New Testaments are conjoined,

like the stalk and the flower. In her virginal longing for God, she sums up all the expectancy of the Old. As mother, she brings that expectancy to its climax in the New. Pregnant with promise, she symbolizes the current stage of salvation history: Christ present in his people though not yet fully grown to mature stature. Both virgin and mother, Mary is what the Church is — a real communion of creature with Creator.

It is from such communion that mission begins — Mary's, Christ's, the Church's. In the third gospel St Luke records that the Virgin's visit to Elizabeth (the first apostolic journey to the world) occurred immediately after the angel's annunciation. The Mother of God thus reminds all Christians that evangelisers must first be communicants. To bring the Lord to others implies that we be intimately one with him ourselves. This is why in the liturgy of the Mass the final mandate ('Go in peace to love and serve the Lord') can be taken seriously only when we have entered heart and soul into communion with Christ and one another through word and sacrament. Mary is the first to teach us the meaning of the Mass. Our first preacher, first offerer, first eucharistic minister. From her pastoral example we learn what nourishes the missionary commitment that enables us to play our part in the work of redemption. It is that unity in the Lord which the liturgy both expresses and increases.

Our Lady's intimacy with her Son attained its highest expression at Calvary. Embracing his self-sacrifice in her maternal heart, she revealed the true nature of discipleship and showed that there can be no participation in Christ without suffering. 'Unless a man takes up his cross daily and follows me, he cannot be my disciple'. In accepting these words literally Mary clarified at once her own function in God's plan and the function of every Christian who desires fellowship with the Redeemer. Her stance at Golgotha, consequently, was *in persona ecclesiae*, in the person of the Church. There she represented all the members of the Church till the end of time and united them in herself with the Son of God who named her our mother from that moment onwards.

Communion with the Crucifed is not a popular concept today. It clashes with the view that the individual is entitled to satisfy his own pleasure and ambition at practically any cost. The cross is still a stumbling-block to some and a folly to others. Over against this, however, Mary's solidarity with Jesus in his Passion is a powerful inspiration for the weak and the sinful. It calls us back to basics. It reminds us that pain is redemptive and that, when accepted for love's sake, it has the capacity to enhance the image of God in the human being by transforming him into a more perfect likeness of Christ the Saviour. The Virgin's silent witness in the gospels speaks more eloquently than words of the wisdom of God's plan which works *through* human suffering, and not apart from it. Her road to Calvary not only makes our journey possible. It also makes it a privilege and a joy.

III. THE BLESSED VIRGIN AND THE CHURCH: LG 60-65

Exposition

As mother of men in the order of grace, Mary's function in the divine plan in no way obscures or detracts from

Christ's unique role as mediator. On the contrary, she shows forth the power of her Son since her salutary influence 'flows from the superabundance of the merits of Christ, rests on his mediation, depends entirely on it and draws all its power from it'. Far from hindering the work of the Redeemer, Mary's maternity fosters union with her Son. True to her vocation she continues to intercede for the human race in heaven as she once did on earth. Her motherly relationship with the world as well as with God himself entitles her to be called 'Advocate, Helper, Benefactress, and Mediatrix'. By these titles, however, she does not *replace* Christ. She acts *in union with* Christ as his co-operator in exactly the same way the Church does, which shares in Jesus' one priesthood without diluting it or diminishing its unicity.

It is through understanding the Church that we understand the Blessed Virgin. Both are subordinate to Christ yet each is intimately one with him in his Person and in his work. As Virgin and Mother, each is dedicated entirely to God as spouse, and each bears children for the kingdom. In Mary the Church not only recognises itself but envisages what it is to become. One difference distinguishes Mary from the people of God. While she lives in the perfect fulness of the redemption, we still struggle with temptation and sin. In this difference we are drawn closer to her in a Christ-centred hope. Thus, the faithful '(striving) to conquer sin and increase in holiness . . . turn their eyes to Mary who shines forth to the whole community of the elect as the model of virtues. Devoutly meditating on her and contemplating her in the light of the Word made man, the Church reverently penetrates more deeply into the great mystery of the incarnation and becomes more like her spouse'. Finally, because Mary has entered into salvation history so profoundly, 'she unites in her person and re-echoes the most important doctrines of the faith'. Therefore when she is preached about by the Church she 'prompts the faithful to come to her Son, to his sacrifice and to the love of the Father'. In the community's life of faith and mission, Mary renews and increases the zeal of the Church by her own maternal and apostolic example, inspiration, and intercession.

Reflection

Mariology has long been a point of contention between the communities of the Reformation and the Catholic Church (Latin and Eastern). There are a number of reasons why this is so. The principal is that which this section deals with, the problem of the one mediator. The question is posed as to how we can speak of Mary's intercessory role when the New Testament specifies that 'there is one mediator between God and men, the man Christ Jesus' (1 Tim 2:5). Even Catholics today become confused when this text is cited as an argument against Marian devotion.

Lumen gentium's teaching relieves much of the confusion here by approaching Mariology in terms of ecclesiology, and setting out carefully the liason between Mary's function and that of the Church. Christ's mediatorship is in no way usurped by the Church's pastoral mediation. This is the first point. We depend on the service of preaching and the administration of the sacraments to know the Jesus of history and encounter him as the Christ of our faith. This is the way it has been from the beginning. The Twelve were the first communicators of the good news of the resurrection. It is upon their faith-testimony that we ourselves have come to believe. Indeed, it is true to say that without others we could never take part in the plan of salvation. Our religion is a family affair. We do not come to God merely as individuals, but as brothers and sisters. So the Church does not stand in the way of Christ or lessen his stance 'between God and men'. Rather it unites us to the one Mediator in a visible, human manner by what it does and by what it is. Similarly with Mary. The text of *1 Timothy* must be read in conjunction with those other passages of the New Testament in which Mary's co-operative role in the redemption is sharply defined in terms that liken her to the Church. Everything that is said of the Church today can be attributed also to the Virgin Mother of God in the scriptures. It was she who brought to life then, as the believing community does now, the body of Jesus. The Church's predicatory mission is prefigured by her witness to the Word made flesh. Its sacramental ministry does the same thing she did when she gave him to the world. In restating our traditional doctrine about Mary in the context of the revised theology of the Church's nature and function, Vatican II not only clarified Catholic thought and devotional practice. It also rendered an enormous service to the ecumenical endeavour by laying down a solid ecclesiological basis for a common acceptance by all Christians of Mary's proper place in our Christocentric faith.

Just as we cannot come to the Father but through Jesus, nor to Jesus without the Church, neither can the Church come to Christ without Mary. In God's scheme of things the Church and the Blessed Virgin jointly fulfil an identical task of channelling the grace that comes when the body of Christ is made visible and tangible to mankind.

IV. THE CULT OF THE BLESSED VIRGIN IN THE CHURCH: LG 66-67

Exposition

The Blessed Virgin has been venerated by the Church from the earliest times. It is part of a tradition which gained impetus after the Council of Ephesus (431) proclaimed her *Theotokos*. Such veneration is entirely appropriate since the most holy Mother of God 'has by grace been exalted above all angels and men to a place second only to her Son'. The Virgin herself approves the filial devotion shown her by the Church. Because of her special involvement in the mysteries of Christ she indeed prophesied that 'all generations will call me blessed' (Lk 1:48).

Cultic veneration of Mary is not adoration. This is reserved to the Incarnate Word, to the Father and to the Holy Spirit. Marian devotion, however, magnifies the Lord, for even as the Virgin Mother is honoured, so also the Son is 'rightly known, loved and glorified and his commandments observed'. Therefore, all forms of piety towards Mary should be consistent with 'sound orthodox doctrine'. The Mother of God is authentically revered when Marian liturgical cult is conducted in the ways recommended and prescribed by the teaching authority of the Church, and in keeping with sacred scripture, the Fathers, the doctors and the liturgical tradition of the past. When true doctrine is observed and adhered to, extremes of all kinds are happily avoided. Then the proper purpose of honouring Mary is preserved so that 'we are led to recognize the excellence of the Mother of God, and we are moved to a filial love towards our mother and to the imitation of her virtues'.

Reflection

In the last section we noted one reason why some Protestants object to Marian devotion. Here we touch on another. In the past they usually confused the idea of veneration with adoration, believing that Catholics made no distinction between Mary and Christ in cultic practice. Vatican II seeks to rectify this misunderstanding by reiterating the theological basis of honouring the Mother of God, and by clearly and concisely differentiating between traditional devotion to Mary and the worship offered to God alone.

At the same time the Council implicitly recognized that in our past there may have been a tendency to pious exaggeration in our Marian exercises, so that at least the wrong impression may have been given to non-Catholics by what we did. To ensure that this should not continue in an age when the Church is eager to improve ecumenical relations in every way possible for the sake of unity, *Lumen gentium* advises us that the liturgical cult of Mary should be scrupulously in harmony with right doctrine. Interestingly, in this short section the Council Fathers use the terms 'doctrine', or 'true faith' four times. This is to emphasize the importance of an intelligent and informed approach to honouring our Lady. Excesses in Marian devotion are not necessary. They only detract from the Virgin's true dignity and the dignity of the one who prays. Although this problem is one that perhaps affects the faithful in the Latin countries (around the Mediterranean and in South America) more than us, we are not totally exempt from it here in Ireland. Pastors especially should be eager to help their flock towards a proper understanding and practice in this regard.

This does not mean, however, that Marian devotion is anachronistic and should be abandoned. Vatican II affirms the very great importance of continuing the Church's tradition of filial devotion to Mary. This is why Pope Paul produced a special encyclical on the subject, *Marialis cultus*, and why the present Pope proclaimed 1987-88 a Marian year with a further document on Mary to initiate our prayerful response to that event.

Striking a balance here is as difficult for some as in many other things. One way to find the proper equilibrium is to read the papal documents closely, to study the scriptural passages on Mary, and to give concentration to the readings in the Divine Office which celebrate Marian feastdays throughout the liturgical year. During Marian Year it would also be helpful to form parish discussion groups where priest and laity together could meditate on Mary's role in salvation history and consider appropriate ways of rendering due honour to her whom the Lord himself honoured more highly from the beginning than we ourselves ever could.

V. MARY, SIGN OF TRUE HOPE AND COMFORT FOR THE PILGRIM PEOPLE OF GOD: LG 68-69

Exposition

The Mother of Jesus in glory is the Church's image and beginning. She is 'a sign of certain hope and comfort' to God's people *in via* to their glory. Christians East and West honour her devoutly. Therefore, although we still suffer division from the churches of the Orthodox tradition, we are united in our common supplication for help from Mary who is mother of all. As she was present at the Church's beginning at Pentecost, so she is with us still. In her heavenly exaltation she continues to 'intercede before her Son in the fellowship of all the saints, until all families of people, whether they are honoured with the title of Christian or whether they still do not know the Saviour, may be happily gathered in peace and harmony into one People of God, for the glory of the Most Holy and Undivided Trinity'.

Reflection

The great themes of Vatican II echo in this concluding section on our Lady in a document devoted to ecclesiology. The endeavour to renew Church life, the aspiration towards ecclesial unity, and the eschatological expectations of all Christians. In unison with these desires, Mary stands ultimately as a figure of hope. This is not a false optimism which the Council expresses, nor a convenient orchestral note on which to finish its symphony. It is rather a genuine declaration of confidence in Mary's positive solidarity with the Church and the churches in their pilgrimage towards the kingdom. Because she is with us, she who already enjoys and signals the success of God's plan, we can be sure that heaven is on our side. As we go on meeting the challenge of present difficulties in this life, the Church's spirit unites with Mary's, who is Mother of True Hope, Protectress of the body of Christ, and Comforter of God's children in every age.

2 *L'Osservatore Romano*, 25 November 1985.

Mary in the liturgy
(Marialis cultus)

There are two reasons why the Church worships God —
to render thanks for the gift of redemption, and to
encourage the faithful to a holier life in accord with the
gospels. From both points of view it is fitting that the
Virgin Mary should feature prominently in our act of
worship. In the first place she played an indispensable
part in the plan of our salvation; therefore, God cannot
be thanked properly without acknowledging the
extraordinary way he used the Virgin to communicate
his love to the world. Secondly, Mary is the perfect model
of discipleship. In honouring her the liturgy places before
us an example of fidelity and obedience second to none,
one that is worthy of our imitation. No community prayer
would be complete if the memory of Mary were
deliberately excluded. While subordinate to the worship
of Christ, Marian devotion is nonetheless essential to the
catholicity (i.e. the fulness) of the Church's liturgical life.
As *Marialis cultus* reminds us, liturgy celebrates the
culminating moment in the salvific dialogue between God
and man. That moment was made possible by the free
and active co-operation of the grace-filled handmaid of
the Lord. So, whether we worship God simply to express
gratitude or to grow closer to him in sanctity, Mary helps
us to worship him better. Her life was a marvellous blend

of prayer and charitable activity directed towards God's greater glory. Where the Church assembles as a family to adore the source of all life and love, there Mary is present as on the day of Pentecost when the Church first came to birth.

Early on in this document Pope Paul determines to clarify some misconceptions about honouring the Virgin Mother. Her cult is not distinct from the Christian worship of the Saviour. It is part of it. This is why the Pope speaks of Marian devotion in the context of the liturgical year which examines piece by piece the breadth of the mystery of Christ. In pondering the meaning of Mary, we meditate on the unfolding of the life of her divine Son. Beginning with Advent and Christmas, continuing through Lent and Easter, and arriving at Ascension and Pentecost, we are increasing our awareness of Christ's redemptive humanity and glorious divinity even as we think about Mary's part in his life, death and exaltation. She is the virgin expectant in Advent, the Mother of God at Christmas, the one who first offers him to the Father in the temple (2 February) and again at Calvary (Good Friday), follows him in his pastoral ministry among the people of Israel, awaits with the apostles his rising from the tomb, rejoices at the coming of his Spirit on the Church. The two stories of Mary and Christ are intertwined; they are one. In the revised liturgy after Vatican II this interdependence of the Son of God and the Mother of God in the scheme of salvation is stressed eloquently in the texts of the Missal, the Lectionary, and the Prayer of the Church (the Divine Office).

Mary is commemorated daily at the celebration of the Mass. The Eucharistic Prayers place her at the heart of the divine sacrifice as the fourth gospel does. Where the memory of her Son's perfect self-offering is recalled efficaciously, there Mary will always be found. Both God's will and Mary's would never have it any other way. Today as then she continues to pray with the community of God's people gathered in the upper room of our parish sanctuaries. The Gradual and Collect prayers, also, remind us of her continuing role in the work of redemption which is extended through all time by means of the liturgy we participate in. 'Grant that your Church which with Mary shared in Christ's Passion may be worthy to share also in his resurrection' (15 September Collect), and 'With Mary may we always praise you' (31 May Collect). In all this the faithful are instructed on Mary's fidelity in the past, but more: they are also encouraged to make her response their own in the present.

The Lectionary

Since the re-grouping of the scripture readings into the current three-year cycle, Pope Paul's spiritual vision of coming to Jesus through Mary is given its most practical application. A rich collection of texts, distributed through the seasons in timely thematic sequence, facilitates a much clearer appreciation of the mystery of Christ and its relevance to the needs of the modern world. Not restricted to specific Marian feasts but spanning also certain of the

Sundays of the year, those texts which feature Mary are now made accessible to the man in the street and his concerns 'in the celebration of rites that deeply concern the Christian's sacramental life and the choices confronting him, as also in the joyful or sad experiences of his life on earth' (MC 12).

The Prayer of the Church

Second only to the rite of the Mass, the revised breviary exemplifies Vatican II's intention to reform the liturgy in a way that will make it more meaningful to those who worship God every day. Here again Mary features prominently in the hymns, prayers and readings that mark the celebration of the seasons. In a prayer-form designed to sanctify the hours, Mary's presence is both a stimulus to zealous pastoral activity and a reminder of the necessity of prayer for such work to be fruitful. The legacy of our best Marian writings — from the early Fathers, doctors of the Church, and the Mystics — is given to us in Matins. Frequently the Mother of God is invoked in the general intercessions of Lauds and Vespers. Compline closes with a Marian anthem as the last Office of the day. No day passes without a recitation of the Magnificat. Therefore, whether our prayer is one of meditation or petition, quiet reflection or joyful praise, the breviary draws on the help of the Blessed Virgin to worship God in spirit and in truth. Whatever the time of year or day, our prayer is duely seasoned with the memory of her whose own prayer was found acceptable and pure.

THE BLESSED VIRGIN AS THE MODEL OF THE CHURCH IN DIVINE WORSHIP

Pope Paul devotes an entire section of this document to a consideration of Mary as a model of the correct *spiritual attitude* that is required to make the liturgy an authentic act of worship. She is *the Virgin attentive* whose faith is totally focused on the Word. She is also *the prayerful Virgin* whose Magnificat bespeaks a readiness to praise God with her whole heart. She is at the same time *the interceding Virgin*; her converse with the Son includes the needs and aspirations of the people of God. She is *the Virgin Mother* who typifies the Church itself as it brings forth in baptism the children of God conceived in the act of preaching and of converting. She is finally *the Virgin generously bestowing* in that she offers gifts to the Father, the greatest being that of Christ on the cross.

Here is the perfect response to those who ask why we should bother going to Mass, or what sense there is in hearing readings from scripture that are unfamiliar and difficult to follow, or what is the point of prayer anyway or even of belonging to the Church in the first place. When we become lax in our practice, when we forget the value of community worship, when we lose our vision of what liturgy is, how it calls us back to holiness, unites us with God, expresses our communion with each other, resurrects our hope of heaven, and awakens the love in our relationships: when we need a reminder of all these basic things, it is Mary who guides us towards that proper spiritual attitude that puts the Christian life of worship back into perspective again and enables us once more to respond to the Lord in the Church with real faith, hope and sincerity of heart.

Vatican II intended that Marian devotion should undergo a change of emphasis, not a decline. In *Marialis cultus* Pope Paul explores what change of emphasis means. In section 25 he proposes that spiritual exercises directed towards Mary 'should clearly express the Trinitarian and Christological note that is intrinsic to them'. In the past there was perhaps a tendency to isolate Marian devotion from the theological centre of our prayer — the whole history of salvation planned by the Father, carried out through the Son, and activated by the Spirit. Whereas before the Council Mary was admired for her own virtue and splendour, today we turn to her to understand how the Holy Trinity reveals the Kingdom through the gospels and in the Church. Hence the Pope advises that all expressions of honour to her should reflect God's plan and thereby lead us to full knowledge of the Son, increase our worship of Christ, and enhance our awareness of the presence and power of the Paraclete. Vatican II's orientation was Christological; the period since has been characterized by a remarkable flowering in the area of Pneumatology. The Church's closeness to Mary should reflect and increase these new trends in the spirituality of the twentieth and twenty-first centuries. Today the Virgin can show the Church how to be a true daughter to the Father by being truly mother to the Son and truly spouse to the Holy Spirit. She is all these things in herself; to meditate on her identity in terms of the three divine Persons is to see clearly what the Church is called to be also. To imitate her life's example, her attitude, her actions, is to grow into that faithfulness which God seeks in those he has called to be all things to him as he is all

44

things to us. The more we become Church, the more we become like Mary, and vice versa. In her, we the Church and God the Church are one communion in the Spirit, through Christ, before the Father. As Pope Paul concludes, 'Love for the Church will become love for Mary, since the one cannot exist without the other' (MC 28). It is this spiritual truth which the revised liturgy attempts to express in re-defining Mary's place in our worship of God.

FOUR GUIDELINES FOR DEVOTION TO THE BLESSED VIRGIN

To help us organize our Marian devotion according to the spirit of the Council and its teaching, Pope Paul offers four points of departure to keep in mind. In each of these perspectives it is Mary's relationship with God and the Church (and therefore our relationship with God and his Church) which is highlighted.

The biblical guideline

Contemporary devotion to the Blessed Virgin should not ignore the great wave of interest in the scriptures which characterizes post-conciliar Catholic spirituality. On the contrary, the honour and esteem we have for her should be inspired by the divine Word, and should gain new vigour and momentum from the Old and New Testaments. Revealing the very mind of the Father under the guidance of the Spirit, the bible is the Church's great light and source of wisdom. As Seat of Wisdom and Mother of the Word made flesh, Mary is most effectively honoured through the Church's meditation on and preaching of the message of the two Testaments. Herself deeply imbued with the Word, she instructs those who ponder revealed Truth, since it was from her womb that 'truth sprang from the earth' and revealed the Father to the world.

The liturgical guideline

Pope Paul's guideline here arises out of his earlier remark that the veneration of Mary should fit hand in glove with the rotating structure of the yearly liturgical cycle as it follows the unfolding of the mystery of redemption. True devotion to the Virgin Mother flows from and leads back to her Son the Saviour. Therefore, it is only appropriate that such devotion should accompany and enhance the pattern of liturgy, not detract from it or separate itself from it. The Pope cites the instruction given in Vatican II's *Sacrosanctum concilium* on this: 'It is necessary that (Marian devotions) should be so arranged with consideration for the liturgical seasons as to be in harmony with the sacred liturgy. They should somehow derive their inspiration from it, and because of its pre-eminence they should orient the Christian people towards it' (SC 13; MC 31).

This directive from the Council occasionally meets with two unfortunate reactions which Paul VI warns against now. The first is the tendency to suppress devotion to Mary altogether in the light of the Church's re-think about liturgical theology. This would be a great mistake. The other is the tendency to insert Marian practices into the rite of the Mass itself — novenas, for example, or portions of the rosary. This, too, is unacceptable. The correct balance can be achieved by remembering Pope Paul's carefully worded explanation of Vatican II's actual meaning: 'The Council said that devotions of piety should harmonize with the liturgy, not be suppressed', and 'Exercises of piety should be harmonized with the liturgy, not merged into it' (MC 31). One profitable occupation for study groups during Marian Year would be to discuss exactly how these two principles might be happily kept in perspective as pastors, people and parish liturgy-committees together plan the worship of their local churches over the present twelve-month of special celebrations in honour of the Mother of God.

The ecumenical guildeline

Given that Mariology has been a point of contention between Catholics and Protestants for four hundred years, it might seem strange that Pope Paul would consider the veneration of our Lady as in fact 'in accord with the deep desires and aims of the ecumenical movement' (MC 32). There are, however, very good reasons why he is right. In the first place, by praising God in the words that Mary used (the Magnificat) all denominations are united through the graced eloquence of sacred scripture. Secondly, since Mary is Mother of Christ she is also mother of all who, though united in one faith and one baptism, have been separated ecclesially through the vicissitudes of history. No sincere Christian, Catholic or Protestant, wants disunity to continue. In the maternal heart of Mary the ecumenical movement finds its very source, for no cause is nearer to Mary's soul than the reunification of all Christ's bodily members. It was for this after all that she stood by her dying Son at Golgotha.

Given the excellent opportunities for co-operation between the different churches and communions nowadays, *Marialis cultus* advises Catholics to be scrupulously careful about anything that could disrupt the improved relations between Rome and Geneva since the Council. For example, we must not exaggerate the honour due to Mary, as has sometimes happened in the past. We should never allow others to suppose that she replaces Christ as the object of our worship. Neither should we stand accused of confusing Mary's unique role in the scheme of salvation with that of Jesus himself, who is the only mediator between God and man. None of these is in keeping with what Catholics believe anyway. On the contrary, our understanding of the Virgin Mary's maternity with respect to Christ and his Church as outlined in *Lumen gentium* and *Marialis cultus* is consistent with what Catholic doctrine has always taught. This should remain the basis of all our Marian spirituality whose purpose is to draw the Church together in union with Christ in a common spirit of gratitude to the Father for what he has done for mankind through his Word made flesh. In other words, if all the criteria discussed so far in *Marialis cultus* are sincerely observed, our veneration of Mary will be in accord with what is truly unitive and charitable. Then, concludes Pope Paul, 'devotion to the humble Handmaid of the Lord, in whom the Almighty has done great things, will become, even if slowly, not an obstacle but a path and a rally-point for the union of all who believe in Christ' (MC 33).

Like the changes brought by Vatican II in liturgy and theology generally, so the modernization of devotion to Mary must be located within the social climate of our time. It must respond to the way we think and feel today, taking account of the needs of men and women now. Spirituality cannot be divorced from psychology, sociology and anthropology. One such change in thought, for instance, concerns the role of women in society and the Church. The last two decades have seen an enormous shift in the perception women have of themselves. Unless Marian devotion is re-structured with these changes in mind it runs the danger — like the Church itself — of appearing irrelevant. Here again as in the other instances, Mary has an important part to play in bringing the men and women of the third millennium close to the God who calls his people to full and active participation in his plan in every age and cultural climate.

The Virgin Mother in fact exemplifies the aspirations of women today in an ideal manner. The modern woman is looking for full recognition of her intrinsic worth so she can realize her maximum human capacity. She desires freedom of personhood, choice and self-expression in order to play a more involved role in the building up of the earthly city. Vatican II reminded us (*Gaudium et spes* 39) that while the kingdom of heaven and earthly progress are not synonymous, the former does depend upon the activity of the faithful in this world for its definitive coming. The feminine ambition, therefore, for greater involvement is, for the most part, eminently in harmony with the ambition of God himself, whose kingdom comes not apart from the day to day work of civilization, but through the sanctified contribution of all the faithful, male and female together. If Marian devotion is properly ordered according to the entire theological vision of Vatican II, in keeping with the sacred scriptures and the best of sacred tradition, Mary will indeed be perceived as a worthy prototype of the women of our times who sincerely wish to improve modern life by their commitment to service. The Virgin of Nazareth typifies the liberated woman because she was filled with the Spirit who sets us free. She is the perfect example of what Jesus meant in his conversation with Nicodemus (Jn 3:6-8) when he spoke of that detachment of the self from whatever enslaves the human personality. Mary was perfectly detached for the sake of being perfectly involved in the work of the Spirit. Her sex was no obstacle to this; on the contrary, it was an indispensable part of who she was and of what she brought to the service of the kingdom. As St Paul says, in the accomplishment of salvation there is no sexual discrimination in the divine plan, since in God's eyes there is 'neither male nor female; for you are all one in Christ Jesus' (Gal 3:28; 1 Cor 12:12-13; Col 3:11). This is not at all to blur the differentiating role of men and women in the body of Christ anymore than we wish to blur the roles of Mary and Christ. But it *is* to assert — as Mary's own story does — that women have a specific and necessary contribution to make in the process of salvation. The Church, therefore, must re-evaluate its position on this question, as it is already doing in the case of the laity generally, in the light of contemporary anthropological trends. There is no doubt whatsoever that the development of Mariology and the revision of Marian devotion as suggested by all the recent Popes will be an invaluable aid in this regard.

In the past our image of the Virgin may have been adversely affected by the poor taste of sentimental popular art. If we ever thought of her as timid, submissive-to-fortune, somewhat doleful and servile, or even impossibly out of touch with what's what, we were gravely misled. The actual picture of Mary outlined in the New Testament is of a strong and questioning woman, greatly moved by feminine emotion, apprehensive about reality, yet firmly confident in the victorious outcome of a life lived in obedience to the Mighty God of Israel. She understood that people gain their freedom not by avoiding effort and pain, but by facing reality with the personal courage and heroic love that his strength gives. Mary's calm serenity in the struggle with life is proof of her own self-possession. Few women in history have ever come near to the triumph of spirit that was hers as she uncompromisingly pursued her most authentic self-realization. St Luke depicts the Virgin of Nazareth as 'greatly disturbed' by God's call. She is fearful at the angel's visitation, perplexed by his words, cautious in her lack of understanding. Later she wonders greatly at what the shepherds say, ponders carefully on the dark prophecy of Simeon, is surprised at the words of the Child Jesus lost in the temple, reacts sharply to his independence ('Your father and I have been looking for you anxiously'), is astonished at his forthright reply and attitude. Such a picture leaves us in no doubt, if we are to read the gospel accurately, that Mary's faith was a lively, intelligent and searching response to a role that demanded of her the full panoply of her personal faculties and attributes as a woman.

To be true to the Mary of history is to eradicate all pious excesses from our devotion. Excesses only indicate an unwillingness to face the real issues that Mary faced. They are a base indulgence in a spiritual fantasy world devoid of the redemptive cross which the Virgin Mother carried in her heart. Pope Paul warns us firmly against this. 'The Council has also denounced certain devotional deviations, such as vain credulity, which substitutes reliance on merely external practices for serious commitment. Another deviation is sterile and ephemeral sentimentality so alien to the spirit of the gospel that demands persevering and practical action' (MC 38). From this we can conclude that wherever Marian devotion leads the faithful to a more active engagement in the love of God and one's neighbour in the normal circumstances of one's daily state, there our veneration of the Mother of Christ is authentic and fruitful and pleasing to God. Only when our perception of the Virgin Mary has been purified through a realistic re-appraisal of her role in God's plan as Mother of his Son and of the Church can we begin to discern the actual place of women in society and the Church today. If set apart from Mary, contemporary ideas on this are in serious danger of demeaning or degrading the status of women by suggesting they can achieve self-realization outside the dynamic and sanctifying power of the word of God in whom all things are brought to perfect fulfilment.

OBSERVATIONS ON TWO EXERCISES OF PIETY: THE ROSARY AND THE ANGELUS

Aside from the fact that these two devotions bear the

venerable stamp of a long and fruitful tradition in the history of prayer, they are eminently acceptable to the spirituality of today for many other good reasons. In the first place they are almost entirely culled from the phraseology of the scriptures. Therefore, to pray the Rosary or recite the Angelus reverently is to repeat the texts of St Luke or St John, a practice that expresses admiration and love for the word of God. The rhythm of these prayers, too, appeals to the modern sensibility. It is of the nature of the mantra which has recently generated much interest and become fashionable in the west. How many books have been published over the last two decades on this re-vitalized aid to contemplation where body and spirit are harmonized through the regularity of breathing and the quiet steady repetition of the key word or phrase that directs the whole person to God? Even more than this, the traditional Marian prayers enhance that sometimes difficult-to-master mental prayer which is discursive and imagistic in character. When recited with an eye to passages of the New Testament, they enable us to focus attention quite easily on the course of the mysteries of salvation through the graphic highlights of the story of Jesus. A most appropriate way of using the Rosary, for example, is to begin each decade with a short reading from the infancy narrative of the third gospel, or the Passion according to *Matthew*, or the concluding chapters of *St John*, or the opening chapter of the *Acts*, or chapter 12 of the *Apocalypse*, and then to follow this up with a decade in the usual way, keeping in mind the scripture text just read. To make the meditation even more relevant, one might conclude that decade with a spontaneous short address to Christ or to

53

the Father or the Holy Spirit arising out of the reflection, requesting a deeper commitment in one's life to whatever aspect of the plan of redemption has been the object of one's thought.

Here in fact lies the superb value of the Rosary and the Angelus. They put us in touch with the scheme of the divine will by the process of recalling the miracle of the Incarnation. Every time we do this in faith, we cannot but be affected by God's grace, because whenever the paschal mystery is commemorated Jesus becomes really present in Person. The Rosary and the Mass have something in common here. Both are memorials, although the Mass is sacramentally efficacious whereas the Rosary is not. Nevertheless, as a memorial each puts us in the plane of salvation in a real way. This is why during the penal days in Ireland, it is said, the faith of our forefathers was preserved by their fidelity to the Rosary when the Mass was outlawed. This fact alone should convince us of the close bond that ties the Rosary to the celebration of the Eucharist. This is not to imply that the two may take place concurrently: they are complementary but not to be confused. Nevertheless, the Rosary is an excellent preparation for the Eucharistic Celebration and an admirable prolongation of the *anamnesis* of the Mass when the liturgy is over. Pope Paul summed up the intrinsic relationship between the two in the following way: 'Liturgical celebrations and the pious practice of the Rosary must be neither set in opposition to one another nor considered as being identical. . . . The former presents anew, under the veil of signs and operative in a hidden way, the great mysteries of our redemption. The latter, by means of devout contemplation, recalls these same mysteries to the mind of the person praying and stimulates the will to draw from them the norms of living. Once this substantial difference has been established, it is not difficult to understand that the Rosary is an exercise of piety that draws its motivating force from the liturgy and leads naturally back to it' (MC 48).

In our own Irish tradition the story of Knock underlines clearly the accuracy of the Pope's observations. There the Virgin Mary appeared in the stance of the priest at Mass, her hands uplifted in a sacerdotal attitude, her gaze directed towards heaven, the Eucharistic Lamb on the altar behind her, St John the Evangelist (symbolizing the liturgy of the Word) to one side, St Joseph (proclaimed Guardian of the Church in 1875) to the other. No word was uttered to the visionaries. None was necessary. The tableau said everything to a people who for centuries had remained faithful to God, even when deprived of the public liturgy, by their devotion to the Marian Rosary. Mary's appearance was surely the finest and most significant approbation that heaven could have shown to the Irish people at that time, as they emerged from the darkness of persecution with their faith intact and strengthened for the new challenges of the twentieth century. Today as then Mary wishes to protect that faith, especially among the young of the country. If the Rosary and the Angelus helped us before, why should we doubt that they will help us again now?

The motherhood of Mary and the Redemption (Redemptoris Mater)

I. MARY IN THE MYSTERY OF CHRIST

This first section is a rich series of Marian meditations based on the word of God in the New Testament. Taking the gospels and the letters of St Paul mostly, Pope John Paul II considers how Mary's part in the plan of salvation can put us in touch with 'the love of Christ which surpasses knowledge' (Eph 3:19) and guide us in our Christian response to that love. His method of using the scriptures directly to honour Mary is an exemplary application of his predecessor Paul VI's instruction in *Marialis cultis* that 'devotion to the Blessed Virgin should draw inspiration in a special way from . . . the Bible as the basic prayerbook' (MC 30).

These meditations centre around a number of key words or phrases which the Pope picks up in the beginning and comes back to again and again. They include the terms 'fulness, 'blessed', 'mystery', 'motherhood', 'woman', and 'pilgrimage of faith'. We look at a few of these now closely.

'Fulness'

The document begins with a reference to St Paul

(Galatians 4:4), who speaks of the birth of Jesus of a woman in the fulness of time. This is the moment chosen by God from eternity when his great design to reverse the sin of Adam would be revealed through his own Son. Mary is part of this fulness. She is fully incorporated into the divine scheme of things. Her presence marks the dawn of the new age which was to transform human history. Through the fulness of her pregnancy appears the one in whom dwells the fulness of God.

This is why Mary is rightly called 'full of grace'. By her full co-operation with the Holy Trinity in faithful obedience she dispels the darkness of the old era, permitting the light of the world to rise from within her womb. This great truth is what inspired the Pope to proclaim a Marian Year. The time between now and the turn of the century is like another marvellous Advent as we prepare to celebrate the second millennium of Christ's birth. As Mary preceded him then, so in the Church now the memory of the Virgin who became the Mother of God leads us spiritually towards the Jubilee Christmas twelve years ahead. Using an ancient and venerable image Pope John Paul compares our Lady to the morning star which heralds the dawn. The light of that star is to be the focus of our attention in the protracted Advent from 1988 to A.D. 2000.

'Blessed'

Because Mary is full of grace she is therefore truly blessed. As she said herself in St Luke's gospel, "All generations will call me blessed'. In this the Mother of God stands for all God's people. St Paul again makes it clear in the

Christological hymn of *Ephesians* that this is the very point of Christ's coming. From all eternity the Father has had it in mind to 'bless us in Christ with every spiritual blessing in the heavenly places'. Hence he 'chose us in him that we should be holy and blameless before him', and 'destined us in love to be his sons through Jesus Christ according to the purpose of his will'. In this remarkable design, Mary is first of the fully blessed, the new creation, the community of the redeemed.

The point of our election was God's determination to right the wrong of Eden. The Genesis story of the fall is the context within which the promise of the Redeemer was made. Ever since, the struggle with sin and death has been the context within which the drama of salvation has been played. Mary takes her place in the arena with the rest of mankind, but her election by the Father has changed the terms by which the battle is fought. Because she is Mother of Christ the Victor, her blessedness assures the Church of its ultimate success in union with Christ over the power of evil. Thus *Redemptoris Mater* acclaims Mary as the guarantee that our faith in God's superior force is not in vain. By the love with which he called us, our spiritual enemy is vanquished:

> The victory of the woman's Son will not take place without a hard struggle, a struggle that is to extend through the whole of human history. . . . Mary, Mother of the Incarnate Word, is placed at the very centre of that enmity, that struggle which accompanies the history of humanity on earth and the history of salvation itself. In this central place, she who belongs to the 'weak and poor of the Lord'

bears in herself, like no other member of the human race, that 'glory of grace' which the Father 'has bestowed on us in his beloved Son', and this grace determines the extraordinary greatness and beauty of her whole being. Mary thus remains before God, and also before the whole of humanity, as the unchangeable and inviolable sign of God's election, spoken of in Paul's letter: 'in Christ . . . he chose us . . . before the foundation of the world, . . . he destined us to be his sons' (Eph 1:4, 5). This election is more powerful than any experience of evil and of sin, than all that 'enmity' which marks the history of man. In this history Mary remains a sign of sure hope (RM 11).

'Pilgrimage of faith'

If Mary was a woman blessed, it was because she was richly endowed with faith. By this gift did the Father draw her to himself and to his will. Her faith was part of the fulness of grace whereby God dwelt within her, occupying not only her womb but her mind and will as well. Elizabeth recognized clearly in her that which was most worthy of honour: 'Blessed is she who believed that the promise made to her by the Lord would be fulfilled' (Lk 1:45). Precisely on account of this total conviction about God's word was she 'blessed among women, and blessed the fruit' of her womb (Lk 1:42). For Pope John Paul, here is the key to understanding Mary in the mystery of Christ. Her faith links her to us in the realm of salvation and makes of her a lasting symbol of what God can do in the Church which believes in the certainty of his ways.

Mary's faith had several dimensions. It was more than intellectual assent to the holy truths. It was also a commitment of her entire life as a human being and as a woman. 'She responded with all her human and feminine "I", and this response of faith included both perfect cooperation with "the grace of God that precedes and assists" and perfect openness to the action of the Holy Spirit, who "constantly brings faith to completion with his gifts"' (RM 13). Because of this, it was a quality of Mary's personhood that was subject to growth, and this is true of our faith too. In this sense her faith was really a pilgrimage, a spiritual journey that brought her through dark and unknown ways. She had only the same assistance that we have been given: the prompting of the Holy Spirit and the presence of Christ. But for her, these were enough. Hence she is the perfect exemplar for those still en route to the heavenly homeland, of the enduring courage and hope required of the Christian who, while holding Christ in the human soul in mystery, still does not possess him definitively while the journey on earth lasts. This is the aspect of Mary's story that John Paul II chooses to examine in some detail.

From beginning to end the faith of the Virgin of Nazareth was an abandonment of self to the will of God. Her journey was to be an exploration of what abandon means for one who is called. True faith means accepting what is asked of the believer even before one understands what that will involve. Such was Mary's story. At the Annunciation she had no idea of what being Mother of the Messiah would demand of her. Yet her 'yes' was an irrevocable assent to the plan of the Father, whatever that would require, wherever it would lead. The Pope speaks of a second annunciation: that of the old man, Simeon, who prophesied for the Virgin Mother the sword of sorrow that would pierce her heart. From the flight into Egypt until the hill of Calvary Mary would gradually discover through the experience of intense hardship of mind and spirit the cost of her role in the plan of God. Her sustained belief in the point of her Son's own sufferings, and her continued willingness to bear them with him, makes her truly first member of the Church and the ideal of our faith today. We look to her for the inspiration which only one who is 'full of grace' can give to the pilgrim people of God in the modern world. Mary understands the dark night of the soul, the heaviness of heart with which the Christian must pursue that journey. Even though she was his Mother and lived with him at Nazareth, Mary's contact with 'the truth about her Son' was 'only in faith and through faith' (RM 17). In this she shares with Abraham of the Old Testament gigantic status in the bible as a pillar upon which rests the edifice of the Father's intentions. As with Abraham, so with Mary: their faith initiated the covenants, old and new. If Abraham is our father in faith, Mary is our Mother. Each was required to journey through the night of trust, following the star of divine destiny. Each was asked to sacrifice their son. Each was called to parent a new people for the Lord of which each would be the prototype and model. Abraham's astounding hope in the promise is matched and surpassed by Mary's hope in the fulfilment of that promise.

Together, Abraham and Mary encompass the full range of God's incomprehensible scheme, hold the mystery in their hearts and bring it to life in the world so that human history itself is redeemed and made into salvation history.

It is at Calvary that Mary's faith-journey reaches its climactic purpose and completion. Sharing in her Son's *kenosis*, or self-emptying, she embodies in her union with the crucified Redeemer the Father's purpose, hidden from before time began. Now the Mother's faith in the Son 'becomes in a certain sense the counterpoise to the disobedience and disbelief embodied in the sin of our first parents' (RM 19). It also marks the beginning of a new response on the part of Adam's race, a new acceptance of the blessing intended by the Godhead for us since before the ages began. 'From the Cross, that is to say from the very heart of the mystery of redemption, there radiates and spreads out the prospect of that blessing of faith', untying the knot of the original sin which blocked the fulness of grace until this moment in the sons and daughters of the couple in Eden' (RM 19).

'Motherhood'

To speak of Mary's part in the mystery of Christ is to speak of her as Mother. Yet her relationship to him was full of grace because it was full of faith. Therefore, her true motherhood refers to more than her biological bond with him as the Child of her womb. This alone would not have been sufficient for her salvation. If it were, we today who are not blood relatives of Jesus the Nazarene would be at a supreme disadvantage. That this is not the case is demonstrated by Jesus' telling comment in response to the woman who cried out, Blessed the breasts that gave you suck, namely 'Blessed rather are those who hear the word of God and keep it' (Lk 11:28; RM 20). Mary was blessed because, among those who are steadfast in the will of the divine Word, she was first. Pope John Paul interprets this text to mean that Jesus 'wishes to divert attention from motherhood understood only as a fleshly bond, in order to direct it towards those mysterious bonds of the spirit which develop from hearing and keeping God's word' (RM 20).

Mary's maternity, therefore, consists primarily in her fidelity to the revealed wisdom of the Son, in being his follower, in uniting herself totally to his mission and Person as the messianic Redeemer of his people. She was more his Mother in faith than she was even by nature. For us in the Church this concept of Mary's spiritual motherhood is of crucial importance. It means that she has no advantage in the order of salvation over the members of Christ's faith-family, the believing community. Putting it positively, the grace that Mary received is available also to us, the people of the Word, when like the Virgin we abide in his word and fulfil his command as given to us in the gospel. Thus Jesus, looking around at his disciples, continued, 'My mother and my brothers are those who hear the word of God and do it' (Lk 8:20-21).

Since the word of Jesus was in service of the kingdom, so Mary's spiritual motherhood 'takes on another meaning in the dimension of the kingdom of God and in the radius of the fatherhood of God himself' (RM 20). She is Mother because she co-operates with her Son in establishing the reign of God on earth. If the acclamation of that woman in the crowd who praised the Mother of the Messiah is indeed the start of 'the Magnificat of the ages', it is through Mary's *maternal discipleship* that her remark is justified.

But it was a role Mary had to learn through the process of suffering, which re-defined her being-in-relation to her Son.

The Marian episodes of the gospels illustrate the various stages that this process involved. Pope John Paul approaches each of them systematically in his meditations. Becoming her Son's first disciple, even before Peter and the Eleven, she accompanies him during the course of his ministry from its very first moment, according to St John's gospel. At Cana in Galilee her intercessory motherhood causes him to perform the first of the signs which brought others to believe in his messianic power. With compassion for the couple at the wedding banquet when their wine had run out, she not only responds to their human need, but causes the paschal significance of Jesus' life to shine forth before its time. Thus even though 'My hour has not yet come', the water is changed into the wine which will eventually become the Eucharist, so that this marriage feast is transformed into a symbol of the eschatological banquet of the kingdom prefigured by the paschal meal of the Church. The Pope sees in this event the extension of the Virgin's maternal role in several significant dimensions. To the wedding couple as to us, she is the one who intercedes as mother-mediatrix on behalf of all her children's needs. To Christ she is the maternal encouragement which prompts his divine mission. To those who observed and believed, she is the source of all authentic response to the presence of God in our midst. To all generations, her words to the steward, 'Do whatever he tells you', inspire a filial confidence in those who turn to her as Mother to find Christ as Lord and Brother. 'The Mother of Christ presents herself as spokeswoman of her Son's will, pointing out those things which must be done so that the salvific power of the Messiah may be manifested. At Cana, thanks to the intercession of Mary and the obedience of the servants, Jesus begins "his hour". At Cana Mary appears as believing in Jesus. Her faith evokes his first "sign" and helps to enkindle the faith of the disciples' (RM 21).

But it is at the foot of the cross that Mary's maternity reaches its truest fulfilment. Her pilgrimage of faith now complete, its destination means for her as for each one of us the revelation of our hidden identity in God's eyes, the receiving of that name of grace which he alone knows. Mary had called herself only by the title, 'handmaid of the Lord'. Now as Mother she understood what that meant. The maternal *ancilla Domini* was never more Mother, never more servant of her Son, than at this moment of sacrifice. More than just a genetic bond, her motherhood was 'in the salvific economy of grace', was the fruit of 'the "new love" which came to definitive maturity in her at the cross', and marked out clearly for all time 'the unique place which she occupies in the whole economy of salvation' (RM 23, 24).

Even in his dying moment, according to St John's account, Jesus was teaching her about this new, spiritual, motherhood. 'Woman, behold your son' (Jn 19:25): not only the Beloved Disciple, but all whom he represented of mankind and of the Church, would be to Mary what Christ was, would be given into her protective care, would receive the love which he himself had received as a child, as an adolescent, as a man. Just as she had been faithful to the messianic mission of the Son in the days of his flesh, had been all things to the Holy Trinity in the scheme of redemption, so she would continue to serve the salvific Body of Christ until the end of time. And in the same way as God counted upon her assistance to achieve the incarnation and the cross, so he would not extend his great work through the rest of history without Mary's service in the new motherhood of spirit and truth. John Paul's reflection concludes:

> The words uttered by Jesus from the cross signify that the motherhood of her who bore Christ finds a 'new' continuation in the Church and through the Church, symbolized and represented by John. In this way, she who as the one 'full of grace' was brought into the mystery of Christ in order to be his Mother and thus the Holy Mother of God, through the Church remains in that mystery as 'the woman' spoken of by the Book of Genesis at the beginning and by the Apocalypse at the end of the history of salvation. . . . Thus she who is present in the mystery of Christ as Mother becomes — by the will of the Son and the power of the Spirit — present in the mystery of the Church. In the Church, too, she continues to be a maternal presence, as is shown by the words spoken from the cross: 'Woman, behold you Son!'; 'Behold your mother'.

II: THE MOTHER OF GOD AT THE CENTRE OF THE PILGRIM CHURCH

All that Mary is, the Church is. Each is a woman chosen to give birth to the Body of Christ. Each is blessed with every spiritual blessing from before the ages. Each is destined for glory, having been immaculately conceived through the blood of the Redeemer. Each is on a pilgrimage of faith. Keeping all these points of truth in mind Pope John Paul concludes that therefore Mary is profoundly and meaningfully present in and to the Church throughout the ages of salvation history. In this section he probes the implications of Mary's ecclesial role in the mystery of Christ by considering the nature of her part in the mystery of the Church.

From Old Testament times the people of God has always been a pilgrim people. The desert wanderings of the children of Israel are a symbol of the Church's journey to the Promised Land of the Kingdom. But because our journey is one of faith it is essentially interior in character. It is in the power of the Spirit that we walk, 'moving forward through trial and tribulation' by the strengthening of God's grace coming from the Risen Lord (RM 25). It is in this ecclesial journey through space and time that Mary is present as the one who was blessed because she believed. In her all the truths of the faith by which we are enabled to progress from one degree of glory to another, are encapsulated. Her traditional title, 'Mirror of Justice", is an apt one to remember, for 'in a certain way she unites and mirrors in herself the central truths of the faith. . . . She is like a mirror in which are reflected in the most profound and limpid way the 'mighty works of God' (RM 25).

This great pilgrimage began for the believing community on the day of Pentecost. There Mary's faith preceded that of the Apostles, went before theirs, and led the way for them to follow. From her unique witness as Mother of the Lord, confirmed by the coming of the

Paraclete, did the apostolic witness draw inspiration and understanding. In her was the prototype of a faith that had been justified by God himself. Because she believed the annunciation of the good news even through the dark shadow of Good Friday without faltering, her witness carried the hallmark of reliability. Sealed now with the outpouring of the Holy Spirit, it was a faith stamped with durable worth. It would set standards for the future, validating the creed of the Church itself and stabilizing that creed in the face of all temptation to doubt or disbelief.

At Pentecost the Mother of God was also with the Church in assiduous prayer. Faith is nourished by the worship of heart and mind. In the midst of that community her unique witness to Jesus was accompanied by a life-style of prayer which awaited with confidence the Spirit's coming. Before the eyes of the Apostles her very presence was a meditation for them on the mystery and fact of the incarnation, an affirmation of the truth they had been sent to proclaim, and an encouragement to their zeal when the Spirit descended with power from on high. As on the day of Pentecost, so also today, Mary's presence in the Church opens a way to Christ that is human, warm and filled with grace. States John Paul II: 'Mary belongs indissolubly to the mystery of Christ, and she belongs also to the mystery of the Church from the beginning, from the day of the Church's birth' (RM 27).

In what manner is the Mother of God present to the Church? As one, first of all, in whose faith we ourselves share. Since her heroic faith-consent anticipated even that of Peter and James and John and the others, so it stands as the precursor of ours. Here we touch on the meaning of Mary in the ecclesial mystery of salvation, because 'it is precisely this lively sharing in Mary's faith that determines her special place in the Church's pilgrimage as the new People of God throughout the earth' (RM 27).

Secondly, she is present to us insofar as the Church looks towards Mary in setting about its apostolic work. She, who first brought Christ to the world and accommodated in her believing heart the Paraclete, is the model of the witnessing *ekklesia Christi*. She is by the same token, personally present in the Church's mission of introducing into the world the Kingdom of her Son. We are reminded by her being with us, that all the faithful, though scattered throughout the earth, are in fact united in a single communion with each other and with Christ in the Holy Spirit. Where that unity is manifested and celebrated and increased, the Church is indeed aided by the faith and prayerful intercession of Mary, around whom the early community of apostles and disciples gathered in eager expectation of the Spirit's arrival.

Finally, the Marian presence in the Church is to be found, says the Pope, in the piety of individual believers, through the traditions of family life (whether secular or religious), and at the great shrines to Mary which have been established internationally by the practice of pilgrimage and prayer. Resulting from her faithful heart, 'first at the Annunciation and then fully at the foot of the cross, an interior space was reopened within humanity which the eternal Father can fill "with every spiritual blessing". It is the space of the new and eternal covenant, and it continues to exist in the Church, which in Christ is "a kind of sacrament or sign of intimate union with God, and of the unity of all mankind". In the faith which

Mary professed . . . the Church "strives energetically and constantly to bring all humanity back to Christ its Head in the unity of his Spirit"' (RM 28).

The pilgrimage towards unity

The Church's journey today, observes Pope John Paul, is marked by the sign of ecumenism. Although one by nature, its visible unity is impaired, and this has become for all Christians worthy of the name a matter of supreme concern. The reason is that the mission of Christ in his members is seriously hindered by the lack of a clear witness to that communion for which the Head gave up his life on Calvary. How are others to believe if they do not first see the love of the Lord drawing his followers into the integrity of the one sheepfold under the one shepherd? The Second Vatican Council has already drawn the attention of Catholics to the immediacy of this problem. To help our response to the Council's call, the Pope now places before us the fact of Mary's 'obedience and faith' as the 'sign of sure hope and solace for the pilgrim people of God' (RM 29). Because all Christians know that *koinonia* can be rediscovered only on the basis of a unity of faith, particularly as regards the mystery and ministry of the Church, they must also see that 'contemplation of the Mother of God brings us to a more profound understanding of the mystery of the Incarnation, (and consequently of) the mystery of the Church and Mary's role in the work of salvation' (RM 30). The scriptures depict her as one who instructs the bystanders to 'do whatever he tells you'. Herself the perfection of such an attitude, the

71

Virgin Mother can still 'lead (us) to the unity which is willed by (our) one Lord and so much desired by those who are attentively listening to what "the Spirit is saying to the churches" today' (RM 30).

She is already doing this where the Eastern Churches of the Orthodox tradition are concerned. Their impressive heritage of Marian veneration is grandly displayed in their rich liturgical practice and artistic iconography. Vatican II itself paid tribute to the esteem with which they have always regarded the *Theotokos*. The present Pope cites the ancient prayers of the Greek Fathers and the Byzantine tradition, and refers to specific well-known images of Mary as evidence of the long-standing solidarity between Christians East and West that has resulted from honouring our Lady. With this convergence of two great sister traditions which have stored up 'such a wealth of praise', it is the Pope's acknowledged hope that the day will be hastened 'when the Church can begin to breathe fully with her "two lungs", the East and the West' (RM 34). And not only between Romans and Orthodox, but also with the ecclesial communities of the Reformation he sees the veneration of Mary as 'an effective aid in furthering the progress of the dialogue already taking place' since the close of Vatican II. With her the Church looks forward to being able to chant in one spirit as well as with one voice her song of praise, the Magnificat.

The song of the pilgrim people

Nomadic peoples always sing on their journey. It keeps them in step and hastens the end of their wandering. So with the pilgrim people of God. Their song is Mary's Magnificat which she herself intoned after her journey across the hill country of Judea to the house of her cousin, Elizabeth. That Mary accompanies the travelling Church through the hill country of the ages is indicated by the fact that the praying community has made Mary's song its own, reciting it each day in the liturgy of Vespers as well as in private prayer. For a people seeking visible unity in a lifestyle that reflects a single baptism and a common faith, the Magnificat is a perfect anthem. In a spirit of joyful praise and thanksgiving it proclaims the great things God has done. It wells up therefore from a specific consciousness in the Virgin of Nazareth that she (and therefore also the Church) has been drawn into the heart of the fulness of Christ, that she is centred in the very process whereby God is completing the terms of his ancient promise. In reply to Elizabeth's warm acclamation, 'Blessed are you . . and blessed the fruit of your womb', Mary's sentiments constitute 'an inspired profession of faith . . . expressed with the religious and poetical exultation of her whole being towards God . . . (adapting) words from the sacred texts of the people of Israel' (RM 36). In her outburst of spiritual intoxication, Mary draws together the Old and New Testaments with their Covenants — the Old prefiguring the New. She stands as a bridge that links the two dispensations, herself contributing to the fulfilling of the time according to the plan of God the Creator and Redeemer. Her joy is prophetic. It testifies to the righteousness of the God of Abraham, the God of all generations. It anticipates the final victory over the serpent of Eden. It points to the life and mission of her Son, who by his works and words would express in terms of salvation what Mary's voice was already celebrating. In her, all the old suspicion of Eve in the garden was dispelled. No longer would that first mother remain deceived by the 'father of lies' concerning the mind and purpose of God in his commandments. The second Eve undid that error by bolding proclaiming 'the undimmed truth about God, who from the beginning is the source of all gifts' (RM 37).

In proclaiming this truth about God, the Magnificat, finally, announces the manifestation of his preference for the poor, among whom Mary herself is the first. 'He casts the mighty from their thrones and raises the lowly'. If the Church is to be one in harmony with Mary's canticle of truth, this aspect of faith will not be neglected. The poor are the recipients of the spiritual blessings of salvation. They are the blessed ones who will inherit the Kingdom. God's concern is directed towards them. He is their Deliverer and Leader. Thus, as spokeswoman of the truth, the Virgin Mother is the ideal of freedom and liberation. In her total dependence upon God she shows the Church how to be truly poor, truly in touch with its own human poverty, and thus how to receive Christ and his fulness. To quote from the Pope's own words, 'It is to her as Mother and Model that the Church must look in order to understand in its completeness, the meaning of her own mission' (RM 38).

III. MATERNAL MEDIATION

To speak of Mary's role in the mystery of Christ and his Church is to open up the subject of mediatorship. Vatican

II's *Lumen gentium* dealt with the question concerning the sense in which we can speak of Mary as mediator, given that, as St Paul writes in 1 Tim 2:5-6, there is 'one mediator between God and men, the man Christ Jesus'. Pope John Paul takes up the question once again in this section.

This is an important area of Mariology in today's ecumenical climate. In the past some Protestant Christians expressed reservations about the Catholic Church's teaching here. However, as the Pope explains, an accurate understanding of the Council's affirmation of the Virgin Mother's participation in the one mediatorship of her Son in fact clarifies for us what Mary's significance actually is ecclesiologically in this final phase of the history of salvation. Quoting from Paul VI's words in 1964, the present Pope agrees that 'knowledge of the true Catholic doctrine regarding the Blessed Virgin Mary will always be a key to the exact understanding of the mystery of Christ and of the Church' (RM 47).

He begins by summing up the main points made in the Council's document. Mary's ministry of mediation on behalf of her children is not independent of Christ's. On the contrary, it 'flows from the superabundance of Christ's merits', from which it draws all its power and upon which it depends totally. The saving influences of the Virgin are sustained by the force of the Holy Spirit. Her intercessory activity is entirely rooted within the Trinity itself.

To grasp what is meant by Mary's mediatorship is to appreciate her status as Mother. Her mediation is an aspect of her maternity. To be the Mother of God is no less a miracle of grace than to be Mother of God's people in the order of grace. To nourish the body of Christ at her breast is not less significant than to nourish the spiritual life of the members of the *corpus ecclesiae*. If Mary has been found worthy to bear the Son of the Most High in her womb through her faith and the action of the Spirit, is she therefore less worthy to share in the continuing prayer of Christ to the Father on behalf of those whom he has redeemed by his blood? To refer to Mary's mediation is in fact to acknowledge also Christ's sharing of his unique priesthood in the Church's sacramental ministry, and his sharing of the divine nature with the company of the Church as the sacrament of salvation. It is, moreover, to acknowedge the Creator's sharing his fatherhood with those who beget children, and the Holy Spirit's sharing his sanctifying activity with all the baptized, whose first commission is to build up the body in love. Insofar as Mary is Mother, then, she is also Mediatrix in union with the one Mediator now in glory, as once in the days of Jesus' Galilean ministry.

In the scriptures it is evident that Mary co-operated with her Son in his messianic mission. We have already referred to Pope John Paul's meditation on Mary at Cana and at Calvary. We have also noted his point that her motherhood was not simply of the biological order, but of the spiritual order of grace. Together these two ideas begin to explain in what sense she is Mediatrix. It is by dint of her whole-hearted involvement in Christ's work for the salvation of mankind. That maternal love at Golgotha, which underwent a profound transformation and prepared her for a new, universal motherhood in the days of the Church, is the basis of her continuing concern for her Son's members now. The same power that was released at the event of the Paschal Mystery and enabled us to become sons in the Son, which sanctified the baptismal waters and opened for us the way to the Father, this power is what made Mary Mother of all mankind, especially of Christ's disciples, and bestowed on her a mothering role in and for the Church until the *eschaton*. Mary's mediatorial function is an intrinsic part of her nature, being of a specificaly maternal charcter, and is in accord with the express wish of Jesus in his dying testament from the cross, 'Behold your mother'.

Intrinsic to the Virgin's identity as Maternal Mediatrix is her complete submission to the Father's plan to give the world his divine Son as Redeemer. Therefore, Mary's special identity begins at the moment of the Annunciation as Handmaid of the Lord. The conception of Jesus did not contradict her virginity. Rather it was as Virgin that Mary became Mother. It was as Virgin, by the same token, that she became co-operator with the Mediator. Such is the quality of her motherhood: it demanded of her that total self-giving which is brought to perfection by the fullest consecration of her personhood in celibate love. In the words of John Paul II, 'Mary's motherhood, completely pervaded by her spousal attitude as the "handmaid of the Lord", constitutes the first and fundamental dimension of that mediation which the Church confesses and proclaims in her regard and continually "commends to the hearts of the faithful", since the Church has great trust in her' (RM 39). Here lay the means by which the Virgin of Nazareth was incorporated into the redemptive plan of the Father, prepared by the Son, and animated by the Spirit: her grace-filled availability to the requirements of God's plan and his timing. Herein too is it clear how her mediation is

77

subordinated to that of Christ: for her, as for her Son, 'to serve is to reign' (RM 41). As she lived that precept to the fullest possible extent, so was she authentically Mother of Christ on the plane of redemption. Insofar as she now shares his glory in the presence of the Father as Queen of the Universe, having been assumed body and soul into heaven, so 'the glory of serving does not cease to be her royal exaltation' in this final era of the economy of salvation, the era of the Church (RM 41). Herself the first after Christ 'to be made alive' (1 Cor 15:22-23) of all who are to benefit from his resurrection, she remains forever in the mystery of Christ, in the mystery of the Church, as our mother of mercy fighting with us against the common enemy until the final appearing of the Redeemer when he shall put all things under his feet. Chosen to assist him in his first coming at the Annunciation, ordained by the Assumption to accompany him at his second coming at the end, can there be any doubt that in the period between she is the elected co-operator in his intermediary comings through the sacramental life of the Church?

Mary's motherhood in the living Church

The Second Vatican Council's great contribution to our perception of Mary was that it underlined the profound relationship between the Mother of God and the Church. It was at Vatican II that the Church became a subject of interest in its own right for the first time. It was also at the Council that the role of Mary was specifically explored in the light of ecclesiology. To consider Mary and the Church together — as *Lumen gentium* did in its remarkable final chapter — is to grasp in a new way the meaning of God's plan in Christ after the event of the Paschal Mystery and to see how his grace is given to us today.

This is why Pope John Paul acclaims Mary as the model of the Church. More, he continues, she is a figure of the *ekklesia Christi*. What is the difference between a model and a figure? A figure is closer to the reality concerned. In a very real sense, Mary *is* the Church, the Church *is* Mary. The remainder of the Pope's document explains exactly how this is so.

Both Mary and the believing community share in the redemption which both alike are committed to extending to the world. Participation in Christ's saving act begins with hearing God's word and taking it to heart, and then proclaiming it to others. As Mary did this at Nazareth and in Bethlehem, in the house of Elizabeth and at Cana in Galilee, so the Church does the same in her faithful guardianship of the word, by her preaching and by baptising. Just as Mary's response to grace was fruitful in bringing forth the Son of God, so is the Church's ministry fruitful in regenerating children for the kingdom. Each in her own way is fecund for Christ. What the Virgin of Nazareth was literally, the Church is analogously. However, the analogy is not simply symbolic. Since Mary's motherhood has passed into the spiritual realm it is even more properly an image of the Church's motherhood now than it was at the manger. In terms of grace, as in terms of nature, it is always more difficult to *be* a mother than to *become* one. Maternity does not cease with the act of giving birth. It really only begins then. Such is what our Lady's life teaches us. Similarly in the case of the Church. If its work were complete at the baptismal font, it would not in fact *be* authentically parental at all, since being a mother in the true sense presupposes a very specific personal relationship. This is the Church's task: to build up a domestic, familial bond of communion between all her children in union with their one heavenly Father as brothers and sisters of the divine Son. Precisely in this is Mary the Church's prototype, its personification. What she is, the Church is, even though the historical and theological terms of motherhood vary in either case. The Pope explains both the difference here, and the congruity: 'Just as Mary is at the service of the Incarnation, so the Church is always at the service of the mystery of adoption to sonship through grace' (RM 43).

This idea is not new, even if our rediscovery of it is. St Paul spoke of his ministry as an apostle in terms of a mother's love. 'My little children with whom I am again in travail until Christ be formed in you' (Gal 4:19). Pope John Paul describes this text as a sign of the early Church's consciousness of its mission and work as a most intimate communication of life, a most personal nourishment of the individual in his growth to maturity in the Lord. As with Paul and as with Mary, so with the ecclesial body of Christ: its maternal, mediatory identity is sealed by the virginity which is more than physical maidenhood, and by the celibacy which is more than the state of being unmarried. Spiritual virgin-celibacy is that inviolate dedication to the service of the kingdom which produces 'a special spiritual fruitfulness: it is the source of motherhood in the Holy Spirit' (RM 43). To be truly Church is therefore to be truly Marian. It is to be in the company of Mary, to have the spirit of Mary, her mind and thought, and especially her prayerful orientation towards the salvific will of the Most High Father, Son and Holy Spirit.

What has been said does not refer just to the Church as a vast corporate body. It also applies to the Church as the community of individual Christians and disciples. God never relates to us as a crowd. He is the personal God: personal in himself and personal in his dealings with us. By the same token Mary relates to individual persons who are members of the living body. Moreover, she seeks a filial response to her motherly love as the person she is, and not as a 'model'. From the beginning of his papacy the Holy Father never disguised his personal attachment to Mary such as a man would feel towards his natural mother. With this attitude as a foundation to everything he writes on Mariology, it is not surprising that in *Redemptoris Mater* he should stress what he calls 'Mary's place in the life of Christ's disciples'(RM 44). Because Mary as Mediatrix implores the gift of the Spirit, she deserves the hospitality of the Christian heart. John the Beloved Disciple took her to his home. Not simply to his house, since he had nothing of his own, but into his care. In so doing he received from the Mother of God that reciprocal care which makes both of them, in the Church's tradition, the patrons of those who consecrate their lives and sexuality to the Person of Jesus himself.

In a particular way, devotion to Mary is coterminous with devotion to the Holy Eucharist. As the constitutive sacrament which makes the Church the Church, the eucharistic celebration is especially close to the maternal heart of Mary. Here the Church performs in mystery what

Mary herself performed at Bethlehem. In union with her the Church establishes throughout all time the one Body of Jesus. In two senses. In consecrating the sacred species through which the Real Presence of the Lord is realized. And, secondly, in conforming the community as the *corpus ecclesiae Christi* more perfectly to the image of Christ, the one Head with many members. As St Augustine said, in receiving the Body of Christ the communicants become more truly that which they receive. Since this was and still is precisely Mary's commission as Mother and Mediatrix — to rear and protect the body of her Son — then it is only right and proper that she should be specifically present at the liturgy, where that process is always taking place until, as St Paul again says, 'we all attain to the unity of the faith and of the knowledge of the Son of God, to mature manhood, to the measure of the fulness of Christ (Eph 4:13).

Finally, Mary's motherhood in the living Church expresses itself in a special way through the status and role of women. This has become an extremely topical and sensitive issue in today's world. Therefore it is very important that the Church should deal with it sensitively and intelligently. In *Redemptoris Mater* the Pope gives a clear orientation as to how this might be done. Mary is the only starting-point that is valid. If we understand the mystery of Christ himself better through her, if we comprehend the nature and function of the Church more coherently through her, might we not also expect to learn from her example the true meaning of feminine participation in the economy of salvation? Pope John Paul does not elaborate; he merely points out that further study is required on this. He does, however, outline the principal aspects of Mary's femininity through which her divine and spiritual motherhood is manifested: 'The self-offering totality of love; the strength that is capable of bearing the greatest sorrows; limitless fidelity and tireless devotion to work; the ability to combine penetrating intuition with words of support and encouragement' (RM 46). In these qualities are reflected 'the loftiest sentiments of which the human heart is capable'. They are feminine attributes that bespeak the mercy, compassion and consolation of God's motherhood, the maternal charity of the Spirit. This does not mean they are confined to women. Men share in them too insofar as they are conformed to the image of the compassionate Christ in whom all the tenderness of the Father is made flesh. However, they are called feminine because they are associated with the maternal nature of women, they predominate in the female character. While that is not absent in men as men, appearing in the form of male gentleness, it is in women that this aspect of the humanity of Jesus blossoms. It would be a great mistake to suppose that such gentleness is a weakness. St Francis de Sales described it as real strength. He considered its presence in the Godhead to be the source of salvific hope. I would rather be judged by God, he once said, than by my own mother. It is this aspect of the Redeeming Christ that Mary underscores as a woman of real gentleness, of real strength. Her femininity therefore complements Christ's redemptive nature, draws attention to it, emphasises it. Such is the role of women in the Church as the redeeming community. In a way that men cannot, they embody Mary by sharing her sexual nature as well as her grace. Not only, therefore, do they have an active part to play in the ecclesial life of God's reconciling mercy today. They have an extraordinary power to communicate the reality of grace and its availability to the sinful, the downcast, the emarginated, the disillusioned, the despairing in contemporary society. The question is, however, how to channel this important resource that the Church possesses in her female members. I believe that Mary herself will help us to be creative and imaginative in our approach to finding ways whereby women can more freely offer their service to the gospel and the kingdom, and be accepted for their intrinsic worth as women. This after all was what the Virgin Mother herself desired to accomplish through her total commitment to God as she sought to work out her own vocation in the divine plan of God's saving grace for the world.

APPENDIX

Marian feasts in the liturgical calendar

1 Jan	Mary, Mother of God	Mary's highest and most cherished title
2 Feb	Presentation of the Lord	Mary's supreme offering to the Father
11 Feb	Our Lady of Lourdes	Mother of healing through the call to repentance
25 Mar	The Annunciation	Mary's total communion with the Word made flesh
13 May	Our Lady of Fatima	Calling to conversion through the Immaculate Heart
31 May	The Visitation	Mission of Jesus within Mary to the world
	Saturday after 2nd Sun of Pentecost	Immaculate Heart of Mary
16 July	Our Lady of Mount Carmel	Carmelite spirituality: cf St Thérèse of Lisieux's Little Way
5 Aug	Dedication of the Basilica of St Mary Major, Rome	Mary Mother of the Church, God's people
15 Aug	The Assumption	Mary, Sign of Hope of Fulness of Life with God
21 Aug	First Appearance at Knock	Mary, the Lamb of God, and St John Evangelist and St Joseph

22 Aug	Our Lady, Mother and Queen	The Coronation of Mary who reigns with Christ
8 Sept	Birthday of our Lady	Chosen from the womb: Patroness of Vocations
15 Sept	Our Lady of Sorrows	Woman at the foot of the Cross: close to suffering
7 Oct	Our Lady of the Rosary	Mary who pondered the mysteries of God in her heart
21 Nov	Presentation of the Blessed Virgin Mary	Mary, utterly consecrated to God from her youth
8 Dec	The Immaculate Conception	Virgin, full of grace; model of the baptized
25 Dec	The Nativity of the Lord	Mary brings forth Light in the darkness

---

'By entrusting yourselves to Mary, you receive Christ. . . . In her the Son of God became man, so that all of us might know how great our human dignity is' (Pope John Paul II, at Knock, 30 September, 1979).